Praise for

"A second life comes to us in music and the rhythms of music, the song and full-throated and quietly whispered tone and timbre of Jeremiah Webster's stunning, electrifying, and soulful debut collection, *After So Many Fires*. In Jeremiah's poems death and machines march in lockstep, a macabre soldiering to the end of being. Ecstatically, ultimate Being answers, and the answer, beyond our most hoped for comprehension, is love. Love, pure and with great beauty anchored in mystery. With lyric virtuosity, Jeremiah Webster speaks into the darkest fears of our time with one foot in the temporal, one in the eternal."

Shann Ray, American Book Award-winning Author of *Balefire* and *American Copper*

"After so much posturing on the parts of pundits, preening celebrities, poets on the picked through street market of the avant-garde; after so much hollow flash, so much essentially genre-bent lineated prose of small epiphanies; after so much, well, else, Jeremiah Webster's *After So Many Fires* comes out of the Pacific Northwest like rain: greening everything, cleaning the language, sharpening the eye, casting a slant-lit wonder about this whole good God-haunted earth, and, most importantly, allowing again a kind of deep breathing."

Mischa Willett, Author of *Phases* and Host of *Poems for the People*

"In these creation stories, these laments and celebrations and soul songs, every life that rises from the perpetual ruin we make and inhabit, every one of us, is mythic. Jeremiah Webster's poems are uncompromisingly aware, which makes their clarity and grace all the more worthy of a new kind of faith, a faith in which you and I and a new one-year-old take our rightful, daily places among the old heroes."

Jonathan Johnson, Author of *In the Land We Imagined Ourselves* and *Mastodon 80% Complete*

Cover: Louis Maltese
Copy Editor (Second Edition): Abby Rogers

Printed in the United States of America
Set in Arabic Typesetting

Library of Congress Cataloging-in-Publication Data
Webster, Jeremiah, 1979-
After So Many Fires / Jeremiah Webster;
1. Webster, Jeremiah, 1979-
2. Poetry

ISBN-13: 978-0-9915832-4-9

AFTER SO MANY FIRES

SECOND EDITION

JEREMIAH WEBSTER

Wiseblood Books

North Carolina

Grateful acknowledgment is made to the editors of the following journals in which these poems first appeared:

Anglican Theological Review: Annunciation / *Beloit Poetry Journal*: August 15, 1945 / *Blue Canary*: Ilium (excerpts) / *Crab Creek Review*: Natural Selection / *Crab Creek Review*: Other Space / *Dappled Things*: Surveillance / *Dappled Things*: He Prayed One Might Know an Eclogue by Heart / *Dappled Things*: Venerate / *Dappled Things*: Faith / *Eunoia Review*: AP Story: Cloned Mules Lose to Naturals in Pro Race / *Eunoia Review*: In Memoriam / *Floating Bridge Review*: Plan B / *The Midwest Quarterly:* Poem Found Etched in Stone / *North American Review*: Scop Wanted / *North American Review*: Machines Were Keeping Her Alive / *North American Review*: Scapegoat / *The Penwood Review*: Ember / *REAL*: Post the Facts / Shoot the Kids / *Relief*: Letter to my Grandson (Who is probably a Cyborg) / *Relief*: Gospel / *Relief*: New Normal / *Rock and Sling*: AP Story: Bear Recovering After Reconstructive Surgery / *Rock and Sling*: Credo / *Rock and Sling*: Model Universe / *Ruminate*: Life Work / *Windhover*: Hero

I would like to thank Laurie Lamon, mentor and friend, for her faith from the beginning. Thanks also to Vic and Cathy Bobb, Joshua and Brittney Hren, Jonathan Johnson, Rebecca Dunham, Shann Ray, Mischa Willett, Ben and Liz Kelm, Nathan Palpant, Hillary Grigel, Jeff Schaller, Nick Dawson, Chad and Kim LaVine, David and Coral Haslet, Andy Hall, Jacob Spaun, Rick and Shelley Engstrom, Jacob Witt, Lenae Nofziger, Clint Bryan, Joe McQueen, Jeremy Delamarter, Aaron and Marissa Burt, Robert Dalgleish, John and Rachel Edmondson, Jeff and LE Lochhead, Asher and Mia Ernst, Matt and Heidi VanSickle, Jim and Lori Meals, Jennifer Johnson, Amanda Mays, and the community of Advent Anglican. Thanks also to the Webster and Allison families for years of support and encouragement.

To Kristin

"There is no image I could invent
that your presence would not eclipse."

Rilke's *Book of Hours*

CONTENTS

II.

III.

Forward

After So Many Fires' elegant opening poem, "Credo," places us in the unalterable experience of having been born into a world that both "falls apart" and is "home":

There is the news:
imminent, decisive, news
of green opulence as the world falls apart.
I build my home
as the world falls apart.

The poem's anaphoric structure catalogues order and disorder, creativity and censorship, darkening and immanence:

There is the torching:
novels, martyrs, torching
of twenty-one centuries as the world falls apart.
I study my books
as the world falls apart.

There is the burial:
dead neighbor, wife, burial

of dust as the world falls apart.
I sing second life
and the world falls apart.

This "second life" is poetry, whose reverberation reaches from *Beowulf* to Homer and on through the modern poets whom Webster knows as soundly as any contemporary poet writing today. The vision of *After So Many Fires* begins with its title, summoning the ecstatic vision of the poet-prophet, the witness and defender whose civilization is lost, whose modern ideals for planet and humanity have failed spectacularly. In his contemporary time and place, as the world continues to fall apart, Webster looks for truth and meaning. This is home. From here, his poems mourn and sing.

The title, *After So Many Fires*, conjures the history of our history. It conjures war, violence, and atomic power. It conjures birth, creativity, and passion. It conjures awareness itself as a kind of morality—the artist asks without asking, "What now?" What to think, what to believe, how to live. How again to build great fire.

In this world where "no database forgives / as the abandoned God once did" (from "For our own good"), the poet sometimes feels himself to be an awkward foreigner waking in a strange city. Here also in this space of disjunction, he searches for meaning. Webster's poems, like roots breaking through hard soil for water, do find beauty's flashes, dark glints, river stones within reach, a coming season deeply felt, the symbols that remain.

Mid-section in *After So Many Fires* is the lovely "Fear Spring" whose title speaks the inexpressible human feeling at the quickening of spring. Webster catches the terror of the frozen season's stasis, spiritual paralysis and even vacuity, at the very first movement and moment of spring. How can it be that the promise and nearness, the immanence and the presence of renewal, rebirth, overwhelms? It overwhelms. Webster's lines "but spring: the ambient chant forever forever / that sent us indoors like a storm" are immaculate in their rhythm and meter, and the consonance that pushes the chant "forever forever" into the last line where faith fails terribly. We are human. We fail to see miracle as we wait for it. This poem's sheer beauty of language and control of form, the urge and pressure of the seeing and feeling is evident throughout *After So Many Fires*, and one appreciates Webster's poetic eye and ear tipped toward absolute precision. Again, from "Ecclesiastes":

Once aboard, appendages hewn,
the body is kicked back into the ocean
for the long swimless dive downward.

In a terrible showing of the slaughter of sharks for fin, for commerce, Webster's control moves language through the Saxon push of fact and unembellishment through assonance that slows the action's aftermath and unites the world of violence with the human feeling of horror: "hewn," "ocean," and "downward." The meter brings Hopkins near, and also Richard Hugo, particularly "Degrees of Gray in Philipsburg," another poem about "resources" and the human cost of moral dereliction.

In the final section of the collection, Webster connects the great fires of western civilization's mythology and history to contemporary culture: the new millennia violence meets Achilles. In "Post the Facts / Shoot the Kids," "the nation's children are taking over" in a way that brings to sharp focus the urgency for the correction of vision and ideals. Our children are brilliant and tender. The delicate son in the poem "Other Space" shifts his gaze and wonder from the aquarium glass to his father's face,

to look at me, seeking
assurances I cannot give, the reason
we reside in this space
and not the other.

The boy sees mystery, another world, and in his wonder, his future flares open. In this moment, does he hear through the glass "hymns / saints cannot teach" (from "Ilium")? Our witnessing of the father's experience is beautiful as he watches his son encounter the world. Yet he knows, as his son does not, that the aquarium is a zoo. On what near day will the boy learn about rising temperatures and shrinking habitat? The poet builds his home and the world falls apart.

In "Ember," the moving lyric that anchors the book's third section, the poet returns to his father's home where "Even now my father listens to God." The father's faith, study, work, and words "burn" life into completeness and love. There is such tenderness in the speaker's memory of grace and assurance: "Eden, cicada, altar / are common themes at dinner," while feeling also the weight of "having a prophet in the house." The poem recalls the lines in Roethke's "The Rose," with the complex father / gardener / God-figure: "What need for heaven, then, / with that man, and those roses?"

In the poem's closing lines, the paradox of "Credo's" opening, "I sing second life / and the world falls apart," is transcended:

Why do I rattle against earth and heaven
as though his mouth holds heaven's ember?
Love is to wrestle like angels.

Like the word of God, the ember is both beginning and end. Both fathers are father and son. The "news" of the contemporary world, the "rattle" of human anguish is replaced by the symbol of first news, first word (from "Ilium"):

a fire burning backward:
ash, ember, flame.

In this first collection of his poems, Jeremiah Webster has offered us something rare.

The poet-speaker resists the centrality of personality for the larger work of framing his life, our lives, parallel to history's human failures, and the magnificent fact of faith.

Laurie Lamon

Prelude

Credo

There is the news:
imminent, decisive, news
of green opulence as the world falls apart.
I build my home
as the world falls apart.

There is the torching:
novels, martyrs, torching
of twenty-one centuries as the world falls apart.
I study my books
as the world falls apart.

There is the purchase:
stocks, estates, purchase
of tinder as the world falls apart.
I sell my possessions
as the world falls apart.

There is the burial:
dead neighbor, wife, burial
of dust as the world falls apart.
I sing second life
and the world falls apart.

I.

Scop Wanted

Suppose the genius
of language
is reverberation,
the way a word *—beatific—*
becomes more than a tick the tongue prattles off
after the sounds have risen
from the hall of the human throat.

St. Ambrose was perhaps the first
to deny himself the pleasure
of reading aloud,
to let a word mean its sound
as we think of a heart
housing an immortal soul.

No wonder
students despise *Beowulf,*
the songs of Heorot
dormant on desks.
The teacher is writing:

caesura

litotes

kenning

as the arm of Grendel

twitches even now at his feet.

Poem Found Etched In Stone

If you could see the morning gather the night
into slight graves behind the trees,
and taste the apple sweet
when swallowed, you would understand
why I did not go when they said,
"We have found happiness
in the city," and sold all they had,
weeping like addicts
when urban machines became audible
enough to silence their songs.

Machines Were Keeping Her Alive

and I began to think that death by bear
was better than death by shotgun, death
from needle mishap, death
from toaster, transistor.
There is the awe
of invention, *Look at this*
look, she said, and the microwave oven
was born.
There is the second opinion
pill given by a surgeon
with sterile gloves.
Machines were keeping her
alive. What grace
to have been born
before respirators and die,
the last breath your own.

Letter to my Grandson (Who is probably a Cyborg)

They tell me you have no use for the eyes nature gave you,
or the feet I called "miracle" on your birthday.
They tell me all identity is algorithm,
that you got a once-terminal cancer and lived, twice,
and that your mind has no use for the technology
of books I saved for you on shelves.
They tell me death eludes you, or you it,
and that you refused a trip to the Space Needle
after a tour in virtual reality.
They tell me the Internet is your beloved now,
that you said Mt. Rainier was "unreal"
the day it erupted for good.

I pray you know
grace abides,
meaning *The Lord*,
meaning *no upgrade necessary*,
in some region
of the synthetic organ
that is your heart.

Not the Future I Had In Mind

Ready for engines to ignite all
two-hundred-twenty-six passengers
in a fiery chariot fit for Elijah,
I take in the view:
clouds deserted by the heavenly host,
bruised from the contrails of satellite
reentry. Engines drone a heartbeat,
a cantata Bach would write,
and I listen to these weird harpsichords
between my ears
tell me turbines rarely disappoint,
that every seat cushion is a floatation device
above a vast Nebraskan sea.

Surveillance

The camera
occupies the body
like another organ,
resides in the private
space that once belonged
to a lover, liturgy,
omniscience,
a god.

Authority

The doctor says
the boy's skull
is too small for his age
according to a chart
I must believe in
with the faith of the same
Medieval peasant
I was ordered to scorn
in public school.

"My son's body is perfect,"
I tell him, "as good
as his soul."

Deconstruction

Scientists revealed
that our sun has been swapped
several times by the galaxy
to give the illusion
of permanence.

By now, five suns
have upheld the delusion
of an orbit around our lives.
"Space is actually a giant salad bowl,"
an expert explained,
"with Earth's past four stars
fading like tealights at the bottom
of a cosmic basin."

My dog and I took walks at night after that,
and insisted the moon was the same
lantern of refracted light
Armstrong used
to blot out the Earth
with a thumb.

For our own good

they are preparing death
for us, death and no room
for a wife to hold her husband,
no street for protest with our coffee,
or catacomb for our children,
the protection of ghosts,
where voices go undetected in the dark.
Can I continue to believe
in the neutral gaze of technology
as algorithms assign guilt
and avatars eavesdrop?
No warning is anonymous
now. No database forgives
as the abandoned God once did.

Exile

I'm waking to find myself in Milwaukee,
forgetting how I got here,
certain it wasn't kidnapping or time warp.
I'm fumbling for the light again,
waking as though my soul gave up on this beer gut
a long time ago, filed grievance charges
and checked out.
Lake Michigan is an ocean,
the Atlantic, or one of five empyreal seas
on a planet not yet named after the gods.

Venerate

At the Radiohead concert
I realize my need for ritual,
even if the icons of this pilgrimage

are a few blokes from England
distorting their guitars
through custom Vox amplifiers.

"Thom Yorke is God,"
and our bodies shake
like charismatic snakes

until only the worship
remains, the fragrance of celebrity
rising above the spotlight's pallor.

Between the crowd's stampede
and the body, between the body
and my pair of lungs

is a prayer: how many
idols were cast
from Jerusalem's walls,

how many rams
are required
for sacrifice?

Basket Case

If competition is virtue,
what of those for whom
the colosseum is vice?

Boys sport uniforms.
Confederate parents call for blood.
Referees, ambivalent, underpaid, maintain
civility as siblings - future recruits - lounge
on the bleachers of a spent youth.

The coach gyrates
quixotic arms like a windmill
as the small boy wanders
the court, hands in pockets,
contemplative,
Socrates in his youth,
trying to care.

Coming of Age

At recess the boys hurled insults like hand grenades,
ambivalent to the verbal shrapnel
Billy "Buck Tooth"
"Lame Leg" Simon
endured (or not)
with uninsured counseling
and the self-care of opioids.

Parents assured me,
"Age brings maturity,"
so I resigned myself
to Darwin's playground,
imagined the honey of words
adults employed
at the BAR and ADULT BOOKS
I was sheltered from,
contented myself in the knowledge
that every Sunday meant forgiveness of sins,
contented myself to join in
when Billy boarded the bus,
stared down the *White Trash Fuck You Bitch* rows

with eyes unable to see

a future without us.

Model Universe

It's all in God's garage
where the dying bulb of the sun still gives light,
and stars gleam off the blond chrome of his fast car.

I hated the science museums as a kid
where every rock and mineral had its own display,
where planets, shaped from hard foam and fiberglass,
hung from an air conditioned ceiling
as though there were nothing
peculiar about the dusts of Neptune
or the twenty-eight moons of Jupiter
perched ready for any who could get there.

In space there is no
crescendo, no place
for the thud of steel on raw cedar.
Yet we go on
with our model making:
tin cradles the cosmos, this piece of string
is history, the line of time
on a spool.

Dissonance

It is grace when the piano arrives,
a gift from a friend. Days later

a technician calls the instrument quality
firewood, a trip to the dump, nothing more.

Hammers hit strings
behind century old walnut,

candleholders predate
electricity, but no music,

no resolve in any major
or minor key.

Is the hardware of war so frail,
can the inveterate couplers

of government
be equally uncoupled

from our remaining dignity?
Can the violent receive such impotence:

Hector's corpse, armor-less,
or Ophelia's lungs left to drown

after, "And will he not come again?"
that I might take solace

in an equality of broken things
even as the wicked prosper?

Too Loud A Solitude

For Bohumil Hrabal (1914-1997)

Bard of those lyric bellows,
who blasted more truth
into the streets of Prague
drunk than most do sober,
you promised:

Inquisitors
burn books
in vain.

So I stack these books, hoard
mass market and leather bound,
privilege none of them, hide
the names from fires
of obsolescence,

wanting to believe you,
that like your body
falling five stories
after feeding anonymous pigeons,
this corpus, if lifted in ash,
will rise again.

34

August 15, 1945

Worse than any wizard
from Oz throwing back the curtain
on his pyrotechnics was the day
god died

and became human
after his dynasty above
the sun: Hirohito,
divine wind, kamikaze,
no more.

The broadcast
went out with the static
like any other voice,
went out from the lungs.

And the believer
cut back the branches
of his garden
until white river stones
glowed with the same light
as the exclusive moon.

II.

Ego Non Baptiso Te in Nomine

When nymphs depart
from the last wellspring of wild trout
that swim against a torrent of melted glacier
where the light of the sun is caught on each crest
as darting flycatchers arch ever and always
and pronounce their final verdict
what symbols remain?

Paradise: 46°47'9.03"N 121°44'15.43"W

The ghost of John Muir rides shotgun
teeth eager for an alpine stream,
an embroidery of birds in his evergreen beard
like the Green Man Moderns think is a myth.

We ascend from a world of no nature:
geometries of granite, trees
planted so parallel with the freeway
they become monoliths of mere shade,

while above, digital marquees
sell streams of stimulation
as though HD
is reality enough,

as though the sweet
catching of contemplation
must be achieved indoors
and online.

At the foot of the mountain
I drink in pure experience.
At the foot of the mountain I pray
until I know the reason for prayer.

Fear Spring

After the six month chill of a fury
nipping the inside of fingers,
after snow the color of car exhaust,
the excess of ice,
after another winter in Wisconsin
we emerge sun blind and restless in remorseless wind.
It was not the snowmelt that scared us,
or the ambivalence of strangers after hibernation,
but spring: the ambient chant forever forever
that sent us indoors like a storm.

Restitution

Quicken the pace and kill the thrush
    for the buds with the blood are dying.
The flapping of one good wing
    scares reverent children
    out of the garden and into the house.

Where is the god of birds,
    of the impossible nest in the elm,
his delight in the symmetry of a wing
    and the parting of clouds
    according to his purpose?

When I look among the complex
    of pebbles and roots
I see only the decay
    that leaves its caverns
    among and on the flowers.

I take out the gloves, the shovel,
    and go to where the body
pulls against the ground,

claws fierce when the shovel hits,
when the earth gives way.

Now the birds of Eden pluck.
  Now they bleed on the palms,
Adam's palms, carp over the scraps
    and fall like stones
    onto the fields of paradise.

Natural Selection

Changing the headlight on a '94 Honda
I look up and see a hornets' nest
perched like a gray mother-ship above
my head; a homogenous hum comes
from the comb interior.

A can of Raid takes care
of the whole colony, and there is now enough
petroleum in the air to choke even the mule out back
beyond the grate fence.

Drones drop stiff, the hive goes
damp, and the thin exterior
of wood pulp and saliva gives
out. Hours later
I shovel the thing off the roof of the car port
and jab it a few times with the sharp side.

Don't mention ecology.
Don't bring up big oil or the plastic rings
choking Pacific fish.

I'm a child of the seventies.

A lead paint, rickety stroller, open socket, Lysol survivor.

Ecclesiastes

The barndoor skate
had a wingspan of five feet
but was unable to escape the synthetic
nets of North Atlantic fishermen
who threw them back dead as bycatch.
It wasn't difficult, those eyes
staring out with clandestine dimness,
the alien structure more aircraft
than animal.

Pelicans, rarely seen, are often hooked
by trolling boats, dragged
underwater for miles;
their slight bodies buoy to the surface
only as they arrive at port.

Sharks can do nothing
but succumb to the thick
chumming off Japanese shores, the swift
harvest of fins and teeth.
Once aboard, appendages hewn,

47

the body is kicked back into the ocean
for the long swimless dive downward.

Here is *St. Peter*,
Vitus Bering's sea vessel of 1741.
The chief mate admires
how suitable the fusiform body is for the sea
before slaughtering the last sea cow.

AP Story: Bear Recovering After Reconstructive Surgery

See the jaw,
the sculpted gums that hold perfect incisors
just before you hit the purple
of his tongue?

See the flawless stitch
around the snout?
This is glass where his eye
used to be, and this is not
really an ear anymore.

After the shit he put his face through
it became necessary to give him a new kind of fur,
durable against the Alaskan tundra
where we plan to release him
like a team of kind mothers.

When he regains consciousness
we expect him to protest,
to claw at his left cheek,
and click those new teeth together

49

under the muzzle as chains scuff up
the stainless steel.

Never mind that no bear
has returned to the wild
without a sense of smell,
or that Otso is buried mute
in a gyre of prayer.

See the jaw,
the sculpted gums that hold perfect incisors
just before you hit the purple
of his tongue?

Fish Fall

An aircraft shipping a ton
of live hybrid salmon
from Seattle to Chicago
suffered complete electrical failure
two miles above the horizon.

Lucky for the fish, someone
had the sense to open the hatch,
dump the cargo, gills and all,
out over Eastern Washington
before the plane slammed into the Snake River
killing all crewmembers.

The fish fell,
(velocity = -9.81 m/s^2 * time)
caught rosaries of light
on soon battered bodies
like the fallen saints
children thought they saw
among cirrus clouds that morning.

St. Francis

The unmoved brute
in the back of his brain
tells him evolution takes care of everything,
that crying is for the lives of invertebrates
run over by a two-legged bastard,
homo erectus packing heat,
thus spoke Zarathustra.

Finding the dog
on the side of the road
(wrong color for the owners
perhaps, a slight limp, macular
degeneration, or maybe
he never learned how to fetch)
is a still-breathing variable.

Carrying the body
back to the car, the call
to a nearby clinic,
makes him believe
humanity is the nurture of lives
nature never intended.

Naming the Animals

When all was undone
   the animals drew straws
to see who would join
   fallen seraphim.

This was organized
   by the snake,
who was clever
   with negotiation.

The lambs asked to draw
   first should lions
be required
   to eat meat.

Reptiles and birds
   broke ties.
Horses went wild when plains
   released vermin beneath their feet.

Blood bearing mosquito,
  when you bit my arm
by the river,
  I couldn't decide

if you had stayed with the others
  or joined me
along the eastern rim
  of the garden.

Propaganda for the Organic Industry

Electric light burns its phosphorescence
down on the artificial sweeteners
in my food, and I use a spoon
made of synthetic fibers to eat
these frosted flakes, certain
the pasteurized milk
in this bowl was processed
in a town as alien to me
as the space colony
I'm reading about in a pulp
fiction printed on a revolutionary brand
of imitation paper.

How can I walk through Manito Park

with proof Fibonacci is right
scattered about like so many

nearly dead hands?
Brittle vein belligerent

leaf, you contain
equations that took

eight centuries to decode
in a flight that strikes one

as the last original move
a city could make.

AP Story: Cloned Mules Lose to Naturals in Pro Race

It wasn't until the back stretch
that Idaho Gem gave in to the Naturals,
lost one for the Petri dish offspring of his generation,
and finished forgettable third.
His brother, Idaho Star,
with a seventh place finish,
gave hope to a legion of mules
eager to make headlines.
Winnemucca Nevada would see the likes of Idaho Gem
        again,
sometimes varnish roan, another day palomino, dapple gray,
        a crowd pleasing dun,
but old Idaho Star, spitting image of his sterile celebrity
        brother,
was led back to the laboratory,
never to run again.

Scapegoat

With a rope around its neck
I pull one of the males (the one
with the abscess behind the ear) out

from the shed and into the dry
light of day. Head low to the ground,
it smells milkweed and grass one last time.

Next to the tree I name it
Azazel, burn anise and palm leaves,
breathe in the smoke before casting my lot.

I burden it, force it
to swallow the list, to take
it down the tender throat.

It receives every offense
offered it, and I cannot sympathize.
This is my way out.

I remove the rope,
and with a dry hollow reed,
hit it across the back,

enough to send it away, to wander
off where there is no water, twisted
horns low before a righteous god.

Right Whale Luminary

Whales reached ocean depths of a thousand feet
where eyes (the size of oranges)
were useless.
Oil boiled from blubber,
oozed on bloody decks
before it pooled at the bottom of every lamp in America.

I cannot reconcile the solitary pitch
of a whale's life, the cold refractory
abyss, with the evenings
of ungrateful revelry it afforded,
or why fear should burden me
when I consider how many leviathans

illuminated
the poems
Emily Dickinson
wrote at night.

Gospel

Do stories fail,
negate themselves,
seek haven with huckster,
heathen, hang their promise from the rafters
like David Foster Wallace: the progress
of enlightened centuries?

Is the world content with a world
where the bones of nymphs, gnomes
preserved in enviable revelry, are never found,
where leviathan has no dominion,
where flowers are only caught, crushed in the machinery,
where Leda receives no recompense,
where Frodo is left for dead?

Here I am, near forty in good health,
educated beyond what is healthy for a man,
deferential (though discontent) in the ossified Cartesian mold,
seeking word beyond death,
word without end ...

procreative torso,

starfish limb,

dormant seed,

empty tomb.

Ritual

Irreligious nets capture silver
tons of ichthyoid offspring
like the time I was in London
hearing vespers in a dead language
not knowing what it could mean
to fish or to sing anymore.

I abandon all expectation
as winter crows fly regardless
of food outside my window.
To wait without hope
is not the same as despair.

I wave on my way past the suicides,
listen to the hum of my voice mosey
off into the maples and by the stream,
where all manner of fish shimmer
to remain in their world.

III.

Introduction to Poetry

Throw a few more lines at the Dead Art —
hope — the Muses hear

Persevere in the prospect —
Ahab was *partly* right

Strike through the mask —
usurp — the eye's privileged station

Nations are in uproar —
so what the hell?

Swell the line to Faust, to the overwhelming question —
add a rhyme to satisfy — Tradition — obligation

Petition the diminished part — ponder —
a world without the poem

You've made nothing — the world —
can invert — nothing — it can own.

Crux

With each night's
dress rehearsal
for my death,
I doubt body
as housing for soul,
the ribcage to confine
holy ghost, removed as
I am
from where ravens bring
daily bread between talons
from invisible
heaven.

Plan B

The fence around the Tree
of Good and Evil

has been electrified

to prevent future generations
from damning screw ups.

That's the idea, anyway.

In the beginning, children
ran their careless bodies

against the fence, straining

to pull a lusty globe
from the hoard of heavy boughs.

Attempts were made to parachute in,

but too many Absaloms
hung themselves in the high branches.

It is now almost certain

children will think twice
before original sin draws a tender hand

toward the wire's white hum.

All Saints

If heaven is rest and rest alone,
(no crowd walking round in a ring,
no juvenescent rebirth of limbs,
or borough where cupidon wear eyes for wings)
if heaven is rest for others only,
that is enough for me.

Is all revisionist (no Word,
but only the word, heard
in a mind housing parietal gods)
that I too will abandon saints and savior Christ
eventually?

I cannot be certain
(if God is subject to the same
subjective law: His being
or benevolence begotten)
I will share the same morning as you
or know where to find you postmortem.

Lord, forgive us our sins

(Hamartia reigns again,

promises bread with *les fleurs du mal*)

Lord, forgive us our sins

as we have forgotten them.

Life Work

In the life after death, poets
are the only ones in the same
line of work. Doctors have nothing
to scalpel. Tax collectors take
up photography, full retirement
for penitent lawyers and congressmen.

In Memoriam

You told me you had once
made love to a redwood tree,
and I didn't doubt it for a moment.
You, last of the Beats, still had the strut
of Kerouac, and sang to the boys
as I imagine Whitman must have done
walking the infirmary halls of the Union.
You knew no distinction between Christ
and Calliope, all was catholic, all
became rosary as we received communion
from our bartender priest,
a Eucharist of beer thicker
than any shed blood.
If I had been able to discern
what you so often muttered
around stories of Auden and Yeats,
I would bury those words with you,
commit your loves to the ground.

Hero

With Skywalker, the hand,
Potter, the scar,

Gawain nicks his neck
on the Green Man's blade,

and between Gollum's teeth
is Frodo's severed finger.

Each returns home
with a wound, a blight

now coupled to a routine
unworthy of cinema or song.

Divorced from all gilding,
the true quest begins.

Such myths are why I cannot listen
to ministers who offer life

without pain, why I lie down
beneath inaccessible stars

as lungs breathe in and out
an unsung portion of possibility.

It is why, in this constellation,
there must be one beyond

the world's *kleos:*
a wounded hero,

the source of each
echo.

Post-truth

Having pried icons from their sanctuary,
and declared the sibyl a psycho,
having resolved all hauntings, disembodied
songs, having abandoned St. John on his cross
and reduced love to a sequence of collisions
in the cerebrospinal broth of the brain,
there is no place left for linchpin
revelation, the protean

nucleus.

All is now permissible:
children unattended on altars,
blood offered to uncertain oracles,
to leave Andromeda Isaac bound to the rocks,
to raise Derridean stones above
the adulterous head and say,
"This is irony, construct,
it will not hurt at all."

New Normal

Redundant terrorism
arrives with the coffee.
Today, a bucket bomb,
detonated on the Tube.
Many injured.
No deaths.
This is called: progress.
Tomorrow, a rented van
will plough bodies more effectively
in one of Europe's dying promenades.

Blame religion.
U.S. foreign policy.
Middle East entire.
Psychos cut loose from a Hitchcock picture.
The banality of an "O, so Modern" world.
I say more. Age entire
slouches toward extinction.
Parents push bewildered strollers.
Children recite liturgies of the dead.
Crow skull becomes a talisman.
Ringtone, sufficient dirge.

And what innocence
when my son declares,
"There is no silence here

for God," not knowing chaos
awaits.

Ember

Even now my father listens to God.
Ezekiel's rebuke of the dry-mouthed multitudes
is read aloud from his study
and scripture fills the house with a history
of wandering Israelites.

Eden, cicada, altar
are common themes at dinner,
and as he preaches each Sunday
through the epistles of a martyr
I have trouble seeing him as mere father,
mere working man; no sure thing
having a prophet in the house.

He believes in the readiness of words
to shake us from sleep,
to move like a winged Christ across the soul
and burn until the work is done.

Why do I rattle against earth and heaven
as though his mouth holds heaven's ember?
Love is to wrestle like angels.

He Prayed One Might Know an Eclogue by Heart

Roman enough to ignore his poems,
Virgil found himself among Californians.
Designer dogs were the first to greet him,
chiweenies and labradoodles descended from the ridge
to welcome his feet as he stood on the sands of La Jolla.

This was not a beach of the Mare Superum.
Virgil knew as much, and relief swept over him
as it must have when he sang by the banks of Mincio as a boy.
Native trees had made room for ice plant and goatgrass,
but he knew this was California, this beach of pre-fab sand.

They came from the east, with clothes that covered their scars.
Californians with slogans appeared along the beach,
all manner of chant and banner along the beach.
They spoke with literate tongues, wove their hair,
wore chic status, wrung young hands.

They were all so beautiful you understand,
with teeth whiter than the lamb's wool of Virgil's youth.
He couldn't tell which one was a god,
for they all wore the golden fleece
when they came at him with clubs
and tied him to the cliff face.

81

Mythology Survey

Dead myths
(*The Rage of Achilles*)
are electric among millennial *youths*,
and divorced from the promise of order
each one divines
from a smartphone
caressed in the palm.

As I fade into irrelevance,
with pop references a century late,
the pantheon still plays:
Andromache observes the slaughter of allotted beloved
as Icarus holds the hubris of high school dead.

There is no ambivalence
when we too become myth
with no Bob Dylan to herald
the broken lives we share.

Literacy

"I don't read,"
a student informs me. First day.
Couldn't this wait, I think
(one never says) until after
the Pequod's maelstrom? In the middle
of some terminal passage from Dryden, perhaps?
Before Winston's "Do it to Julia!" Section 3. Chapter 5.
My vote for reliable horror in prose.

No. This is preemptive.
Prehistoric in its disregard
for what a future of books might hold.
Pre-syllabus even, which merely ticks me off.
So I think about reading
(the class is staring now)
in a world where the prerogatives
of perfect teeth, health care,
copulation, and consumerism
eclipse the fact that we all die anyway.
And I wonder, save for books,

who can warn us of the innate catastrophe?
Who can rise from the ether and say,

I understand.
I read you.

Nostalgia:

to be alive when smoking couldn't kill you,
around for those afternoons when children ran
after DDT trucks as they sprayed their glow out over the
      lawns.

to have my teeth filled with amalgam
and a deep shelter with rows of asparagus and rhubarb
ready for fallout.

to admire Europe's endorsement of
phrenology, bloodletting, and child labor.

to finance a shipment of spices from Burma
for cinnamon desserts on the spoons of aristocrats.

to believe colonialism and chamber pots
are the pinnacle of civilization.

to worship in the halls of Dionysus
and labor under the ubiquitous crest of Caesar.

to build aqueducts, canals
brimming with lead and madness
as water fills the kitchen sinks of Carthage.

Post the Facts / Shoot the Kids

At first, a fifth grader, smarter than the Smithsonian, noticed that the Precambrian had been misrepresented, misnamed among the granite halls, the absolute exhibit of trilobites, the row of official postcards, and the quantifiable cost of admission, adding insult to a bleak prehistory. Thirteen-year-old Nestor, devising his own brand of cosmic motion, declared NASA had miscalculated the odds that Toutatis asteroids would collide with the earth, swab off the coastlines and close the sun indefinitely. 2048. If asteroids arrive, Nestor will see them through eyes that are forty-one years old. The museum has a perfect skeleton of Velociraptor (complete with the same ragged claws he used in *Jurassic Park* to tear into geneticists). A child asks the curator: professional, hell, he's wearing a badge, how many of these bones were actually dug up from the ground, carbon dated, proven to be artifacts that bitched above the hills of what is now the Gobi desert. The curator cannot answer. Like a minor coup d'état, the nation's children are taking over.

Annunciation

Against the privilege of tedium
(getting repairs done on the truck,
waiting for the webpage to load,
another meeting hosted by Gorgias)
angels provide another glimpse
of the first century God
I believe will return.
It is never how I expect:
Christ plays in ten thousand places.[1]
It is a mercy that knows
I do not belong in Elysium,
am not ready for beauty to define
the routine of days and months and years.
It is the same mercy that said,
"Do not be afraid,"
at the Annunciation.
Mary felt the body of God
stir in her womb and asked,
"Who can endure such love?"

---

[1] See Hopkins: "As Kingfishers Catch Fire"

Reprieve

Grandparents insisted,
as though this miracle
of modern science might induce
forgetfulness along with the absence
of a grandson.

But you, stranger
who is my mother,
had other plans.

You tell me you prayed
—Lord, I am not worthy
but speak the word only—,[2]
read Aristotle long enough
to see the oak within the acorn,
and defied the fifth commandment long enough
for me to perceive, thirty-five years later,
how articulate love can be
when a family calls for death.

---

[2] See Eliot: "Ash Wednesday"

Other Space

By the glass, by the portal,
by the water's window, by the pane
is my boy, having positioned his stroller
by the aquatic gate, I stand and watch
his eyes mimic the walleye,
his mouth become the bass mouth,
his body go still as the scales that hang
in the care of Pisces before us.
He breaks his gaze
to look at me, seeking
assurances I cannot give, the reason
we reside in this space
and not the other.

Birthday

You have no memory
as we think of it, only hunger
when Mother is away, mirth
before a familiar face, fatigue
when sleep eludes you, and anger
when instinct unleashes your id upon the universe.

A Milky Way of synapses in your brain
will grow to 15,000 per neuron before
your next birthday, but you will not
remember this one. Autumnal light stretches
its shadows into the impartial remains of summer,
as the same birds I saw last year (I'm sure of it)
fly south.

I make you a cake from scratch,
light one candle, sing
your favorite song.

In the dream

there is no time to question
the woman who asks,
"Is this your dead baby?"

I look at the daughter
in her arms, and say, "Yes,
thank you, we had lost hope."

"I've always wanted
to be a mother," she says.
"Okay if I take this one
off your hands?"

Off my hands, fine,
but you cannot know
the number of terrible chambers
where the memories of children reside,
the regions from which we can never wake.

Faith

I dig the hole, claw soil, cut roots
with the knife until there is room
for the ring box we placed you in.
You are buried, the size of a pearl,
by the river where ten years ago
we decided marriage and children
were worth it. *What is her name?*
I ask above the current. *Faith,* your
Mother says, *It was always a girl.*

After So Many Fires

In this unmerited bed
I have no consolation

for a dying civilization,
no moors for our survival.

Before the dream:
voices tell me Anchises

(carried from the burning city
only to be carried into Hades)

waits for his vision to convict
illiterate citizens, as the dead

curse an afterlife of words
that must be read.

If only Aeneas had chosen the horn gate
and not the lies of ivory.

Easy blame, when it is I
who choose the Lethe over Latin

and the ignorance of sleep
after so many fires.

Postlude

Ilium

*But thou, O Daniel, shut up the words, and seal the book,
even to the time of the end: many shall run to and fro, and
knowledge shall be increased.*
Daniel 12:4

*"What is love? What is creation? What is longing? What is
a star?" thus asks the last man, and he blinks.*
Nietzsche

Far enough back
all was born of fire.

See how ordinary
the Pangaea becomes

when home is used
to describe it?

We begin with the silent
prayer

of stromatolites
as coastlines

shimmer
like strings.

I have no words to sink
below a sea with no fire,

but perhaps you can begin
naming these familiar hills.

* * * *

Mortar was left to dry on the trowel
the day we threw down shovel, pick,
left wheelbarrows to bake in the mud,
saw the moon in broad daylight
appear from behind the mountain
before being flung to the sea.
As boys throw stones from a sling,
so the moon flew from its circuit to boil

in the space of the sea.
Why downcast my soul?
Why marvel at the hour of Earth's unraveling?
Even the experts forecasted as much: the terminal
path of empyrean forms.

God is the first
mover, the second
to return, and the third
authority among Moderns.
There is only fear
when the earth gives
way and the mountains fall
on our freeways and interstates.
He begged for the rough rind
before juice could dry
from her mouth and chin.
She asked for a cherry pit
to suck on and survey the landscape.
The shore gave
way under waves
as a split sun
lit plankton and spare parts

from deserted ships.
They gathered antiques,
dug beneath the remains
of a once proud no longer nation.
As cutworms, imperceptible
from the air, feed off the underbelly
of a leaf, so this Adam, this Eve, subsisted
on ruins.

* * * *

Thesis

Behold, the drunk whispers
as he wanders the streets.
City of Dis, I love you.
I live among your citizens
and praise each one as they pass,
faces flush after meals
on the waterfront.
People stare at passing human
traffic mute to themselves and
others. People talk and wonder
why no one listens.

See the world in your halls,

the vast diversity

of loneliness,

the moment on the metro

when all was silent save

for the clanking of metal against warm bodies,

strangers all texting below the radiant light,

passing all stops wordless to slouch (like shepherds)

over the private miracle:

the incarnate screen.

Gaze with me now,

coliseum, pyramid, gaunt cathedral,

climb my stairs beg skyscrapers, the radio towers reaching

      in desperation.

Nature lies prostrate before your electric defiance.

Construction sites, hoarse workers, steel, wood, brick, bellow

      the NEW

with brittle voices.

Praise the promise.

Drink to towers.

Receive this wine.

Antithesis

We'll have plenty to eat,
Mother? the child asks.
With reverence, she rests
a hand on the generator
for when the lights go out.

One pen for the meat birds.
One pen for the cow.
One pen for heirloom seed.
One pen for the sow.

Water is drawn from wells,
purified through activated carbon filters.
Fiber optic lines run for miles,
the monthly funds funneled in
from urban banks.

Out on the hills, toiling
with able hands, a father builds

his monument.

With those he loves indoors,

he works until palms blister.

His assurance: the plateau

of a world defined by

away from,

further out,

better than,

not that.

* * * *

At the coronation of a new century

having embraced all that is animal in us,

I say praise to caves and waterways,

arid plains below the spiral of evergreens

that tell us otherwise.

I am tired of the modern dispensation:

syphilis and vodka,

self-esteem and caffeine,

of amphetamines that rattle my neighbor's soul

while the world waits,

in rote expectation,
for the earth to take us under,
and drown all
hope, and feed all
gall, and never
bear fruit.

Great new, grand new, imperial
boredom. The setting down of words
I have heard before,
the old preoccupation of Romans,
mouths raised to a wordless wine god.

And from the cliffs they go down
and dance down by the river,
leaving the hides of oranges
after sucking them dry
among dryadic birch.

* * * *

I fear some future upheaval
the Heraclitian promise

stone age reborn
the broken

machine digital
diversion no longer

understood or cared
for algorithmic

chicken bones
a revised

call for blood
priestly and presiding

over the world again
another Delphi

to endure
the weight of a stone

tied to a chain tied to a foot
for I looked and behold

a fire burning backward:
ash, ember, flame.

* * * *

Why do I return to Ilium
to watch waves pull bloodless bodies
back toward the Aegean mouth of Poseidon,
where fish reduce sons to skulls
no father could recognize?

    Black ships draw back with their dead
    as towers fall back on the earth.

Fire that bound
  Prometheus is pulled
back to heaven.

The microchip
  prepares the way
of the Lord

for stone, wheel, flint
  against the darkness,
a darkness

monotone
  when it burns with light
from a brand.

        Black ships draw back with their dead
        as towers fall back on the earth.

Faustus, Faustus,
why have you left us,

why do your children insist and lead us
by the amber light of cigarettes?

The devil you left is loosed
upon an earth without belief.

The devil's altars
are obsidian, iron.

I hear children
beneath the empty corn stalks.

Children crawl
beneath the empty corn stalks.

May they keep still
when trenches fill with rain.

May they forgive the collapse
of each constellation.

And though each generation
carries the promise of apocalypse

let us sing hymns
saints cannot teach,

stoke fire from fallen branches
a little while longer.

Wiseblood Books is grateful to be able to give *After So Many Fires* a second sailing. When Anchor and Plume announced that they needed to close their harbor, we simply could not bear to see this collection of poems peter out and sink, remaining only in memory—as if a mirage, a buoy placed where it dropped into the deep. The poems in this book and the voice they achieve make a significant contribution to the fools errand of literary vessels of considerable craft that keep asking—and at times answering anew—the eternal questions.

Joshua Hren,
Editor in Chief of Wiseblood Books
2018

Jeremiah Webster teaches literature and writing at Northwest University in Kirkland, Washington. He has written critical introductions for the work of T.S. Eliot (*Paradise in The Waste Land*) and W.B. Yeats (*A Rumor of Soul: The Poetry of W.B. Yeats*), both published by Wiseblood Books. *After So Many Fires* is his first collection of poetry.

Made in the
USA
Columbia, SC